CAR SERVICE CONTROL BOOK

Sueltz Books INTERNATIONAL

A bestseller in Germany ... now also in English

... auch erhältlich

BoD - Books on Demand
Norderstedt   GERMANY

Bibliografische Information durch die Deutsche Nationalbibliothek
Die Deutsche Nationalbibliothek verzeichnet diese Publikation
in der Deutschen Nationalbibliografie; detaillierte bibliografische
Daten sind im Internet über http://dnb.dnb.de abrufbar.

A car with service documentation can have more value.
If the service booklet has been lost or is fully described,
this service book serves as a replacement.

© 2021 Uwe H. Sueltz, Germany
Herstellung und Verlag:
BoD – Books on Demand, Norderstedt
ISBN 9-78375-4-31068-7

VEHICLE DATA

CAR BRAND _____

CAR TYPE/MODEL _____

IDENTIFICATION NUMBER _____

CAR REGISTRATION _____

COLOUR _____

LICENSE PLATE AND PHOTO

EXTRA WORK _____ AIR PRESSURE

_____

_____

_____

☐ PARKING CONTROL ☐ UPDATE NAVIGATION ☐ MEASURE AXES ☐ INTERIOR CLEANING

AUTO BODY WORK ☐ NEW PARTS ☐ REPAIRED

_____

_____

_____

_____

_____

_____

☐ MOTOR TIMING BELT ☐ AIR CONDITIONING ☐ LIGHTING _____

DATE _____   MILES OR
                                 KILOMETERS _____   ☐ REPAIR

SERVICE REPORT

☐ INSPECTION

☐ MAINTENANCE

☐ SERVICE   ☐ BIG   ☐ SMALL   ☐ ENTER EXTRA
                                            WORK ABOVE

☐ ENGINE OIL CHANGE/BRAND/VISCOSITY _____

☐ OIL FILTER CHANGE/BRAND _____

☐ ENGINE OIL CONTROL   ☐ OKAY   ☐ REFILLED   _____

☐ TRANSMISSION ÖL   ☐ OKAY   ☐ EXCHANGED _____
  CONTROL

☐ SPARK PLUGS   ☐ CONTROL OKAY   ☐ EXCHANGED _____

☐ GLOW PLUGS   ☐ CONTROL OKAY   ☐ EXCHANGED _____

☐ BRAKES   ☐ CONTROL OKAY   ☐ REPAIRED   ☐ EXCHANGED _____

☐ BRAKE FLUID   ☐ CONTROL OKAY   ☐ EXCHANGED _____

☐ COOLANT   ☐ CONTROL OKAY   ☐ EXCHANGED _____

☐ MORE WORK _____

DATE OF NEXT SERVICE _____
OR MILES/KILOMETERS _____

STAMP

SIGNATURE _____

EXTRA WORK _____ **AIR PRESSURE**

_____

_____

☐ **PARKING CONTROL** ☐ **UPDATE NAVIGATION** ☐ **MEASURE AXES** ☐ **INTERIOR CLEANING**

AUTO BODY WORK ☐ **NEW PARTS** ☐ **REPAIRED**

_____

_____

_____

_____

_____

_____

☐ **MOTOR TIMING BELT** ☐ **AIR CONDITIONING** ☐ **LIGHTING** _____

DATE _____   MILES OR KILOMETERS _____

☐ REPAIR

☐ INSPECTION

SERVICE REPORT

☐ MAINTENANCE

☐ SERVICE   ☐ BIG   ☐ SMALL   ☐ ENTER EXTRA WORK ABOVE

☐ ENGINE OIL CHANGE/BRAND/VISCOSITY _____

☐ OIL FILTER CHANGE/BRAND _____

☐ ENGINE OIL CONTROL   ☐ OKAY   ☐ REFILLED _____

☐ TRANSMISSION ÖL CONTROL   ☐ OKAY   ☐ EXCHANGED _____

☐ SPARK PLUGS   ☐ CONTROL OKAY   ☐ EXCHANGED _____

☐ GLOW PLUGS   ☐ CONTROL OKAY   ☐ EXCHANGED _____

☐ BRAKES   ☐ CONTROL OKAY   ☐ REPAIRED   ☐ EXCHANGED _____

☐ BRAKE FLUID   ☐ CONTROL OKAY   ☐ EXCHANGED _____

☐ COOLANT   ☐ CONTROL OKAY   ☐ EXCHANGED _____

☐ MORE WORK _____

DATE OF NEXT SERVICE _____
OR MILES/KILOMETERS _____

STAMP

SIGNATURE _____

EXTRA WORK _____ **AIR PRESSURE**

_____

_____

_____

☐ **PARKING CONTROL**   ☐ **UPDATE NAVIGATION**   ☐ **MEASURE AXES**   ☐ **INTERIOR CLEANING**

AUTO BODY WORK   ☐ **NEW PARTS**   ☐ **REPAIRED**

_____

_____

_____

_____

_____

☐ **MOTOR TIMING BELT**   ☐ **AIR CONDITIONING**   ☐ **LIGHTING** _____

DATE _____ MILES OR KILOMETERS _____

☐ REPAIR

SERVICE REPORT

☐ INSPECTION

☐ MAINTENANCE

☐ SERVICE   ☐ BIG   ☐ SMALL   ☐ ENTER EXTRA WORK ABOVE

☐ ENGINE OIL CHANGE/BRAND/VISCOSITY _____

☐ OIL FILTER CHANGE/BRAND _____

☐ ENGINE OIL CONTROL   ☐ OKAY   ☐ REFILLED _____

☐ TRANSMISSION ÖL CONTROL   ☐ OKAY   ☐ EXCHANGED _____

☐ SPARK PLUGS   ☐ CONTROL OKAY   ☐ EXCHANGED _____

☐ GLOW PLUGS   ☐ CONTROL OKAY   ☐ EXCHANGED _____

☐ BRAKES   ☐ CONTROL OKAY   ☐ REPAIRED   ☐ EXCHANGED _____

☐ BRAKE FLUID   ☐ CONTROL OKAY   ☐ EXCHANGED _____

☐ COOLANT   ☐ CONTROL OKAY   ☐ EXCHANGED _____

☐ MORE WORK _____

DATE OF NEXT SERVICE _____
OR MILES/KILOMETERS _____

SIGNATURE _____

STAMP

EXTRA WORK _____ **AIR PRESSURE**

_____

_____

_____

☐ **PARKING CONTROL** ☐ **UPDATE NAVIGATION** ☐ **MEASURE AXES** ☐ **INTERIOR CLEANING**

AUTO BODY WORK ☐ **NEW PARTS** ☐ **REPAIRED**

_____

_____

_____

_____

_____

_____

☐ **MOTOR TIMING BELT** ☐ **AIR CONDITIONING** ☐ **LIGHTING** _____

DATE _____ MILES OR KILOMETERS _____

☐ REPAIR

☐ INSPECTION

SERVICE REPORT

☐ MAINTENANCE

☐ SERVICE   ☐ BIG   ☐ SMALL   ☐ ENTER EXTRA WORK ABOVE

☐ ENGINE OIL CHANGE/BRAND/VISCOSITY _____

☐ OIL FILTER CHANGE/BRAND _____

☐ ENGINE OIL CONTROL   ☐ OKAY   ☐ REFILLED _____

☐ TRANSMISSION ÖL CONTROL   ☐ OKAY   ☐ EXCHANGED _____

☐ SPARK PLUGS   ☐ CONTROL OKAY   ☐ EXCHANGED _____

☐ GLOW PLUGS   ☐ CONTROL OKAY   ☐ EXCHANGED _____

☐ BRAKES   ☐ CONTROL OKAY   ☐ REPAIRED   ☐ EXCHANGED _____

☐ BRAKE FLUID   ☐ CONTROL OKAY   ☐ EXCHANGED _____

☐ COOLANT   ☐ CONTROL OKAY   ☐ EXCHANGED _____

☐ MORE WORK _____

DATE OF NEXT SERVICE _____
OR MILES/KILOMETERS _____

STAMP

SIGNATURE _____

EXTRA WORK _____ **AIR PRESSURE**

_____

_____

_____

☐ **PARKING CONTROL**   ☐ **UPDATE NAVIGATION**   ☐ **MEASURE AXES**   ☐ **INTERIOR CLEANING**

AUTO BODY WORK   ☐ **NEW PARTS**   ☐ **REPAIRED**

_____

_____

_____

_____

_____

_____

☐ **MOTOR TIMING BELT**   ☐ **AIR CONDITIONING**   ☐ **LIGHTING** _____

DATE _____ MILES OR KILOMETERS _____

☐ REPAIR

☐ INSPECTION

SERVICE REPORT

☐ MAINTENANCE

☐ SERVICE   ☐ BIG   ☐ SMALL   ☐ ENTER EXTRA WORK ABOVE

☐ ENGINE OIL CHANGE/BRAND/VISCOSITY _____

☐ OIL FILTER CHANGE/BRAND _____

☐ ENGINE OIL CONTROL   ☐ OKAY   ☐ REFILLED _____

☐ TRANSMISSION ÖL CONTROL   ☐ OKAY   ☐ EXCHANGED _____

☐ SPARK PLUGS   ☐ CONTROL OKAY   ☐ EXCHANGED _____

☐ GLOW PLUGS   ☐ CONTROL OKAY   ☐ EXCHANGED _____

☐ BRAKES   ☐ CONTROL OKAY   ☐ REPAIRED   ☐ EXCHANGED _____

☐ BRAKE FLUID   ☐ CONTROL OKAY   ☐ EXCHANGED _____

☐ COOLANT   ☐ CONTROL OKAY   ☐ EXCHANGED _____

☐ MORE WORK _____

DATE OF NEXT SERVICE OR MILES/KILOMETERS _____

SIGNATURE _____

STAMP

EXTRA WORK _____ **AIR PRESSURE**

_____

_____

_____

☐ **PARKING CONTROL** ☐ **UPDATE NAVIGATION** ☐ **MEASURE AXES** ☐ **INTERIOR CLEANING**

AUTO BODY WORK ☐ **NEW PARTS** ☐ **REPAIRED**

_____

_____

_____

_____

_____

_____

☐ **MOTOR TIMING BELT** ☐ **AIR CONDITIONING** ☐ **LIGHTING** _____

DATE _____ MILES OR KILOMETERS _____

☐ REPAIR

SERVICE REPORT

☐ INSPECTION

☐ MAINTENANCE

☐ SERVICE   ☐ BIG   ☐ SMALL ☐ ENTER EXTRA WORK ABOVE

☐ ENGINE OIL CHANGE/BRAND/VISCOSITY _____

☐ OIL FILTER CHANGE/BRAND _____

☐ ENGINE OIL CONTROL   ☐ OKAY ☐ REFILLED _____

☐ TRANSMISSION ÖL CONTROL   ☐ OKAY ☐ EXCHANGED _____

☐ SPARK PLUGS   ☐ CONTROL OKAY ☐ EXCHANGED _____

☐ GLOW PLUGS   ☐ CONTROL OKAY ☐ EXCHANGED _____

☐ BRAKES   ☐ CONTROL OKAY ☐ REPAIRED   ☐ EXCHANGED _____

☐ BRAKE FLUID   ☐ CONTROL OKAY ☐ EXCHANGED _____

☐ COOLANT   ☐ CONTROL OKAY ☐ EXCHANGED _____

☐ MORE WORK _____

DATE OF NEXT SERVICE ─────────────
OR MILES/KILOMETERS ─────────────

STAMP

SIGNATURE _____

EXTRA WORK _____ AIR PRESSURE

_____

_____

_____

☐ PARKING CONTROL ☐ UPDATE NAVIGATION ☐ MEASURE AXES ☐ INTERIOR CLEANING

AUTO BODY WORK ☐ NEW PARTS ☐ REPAIRED

_____

_____

_____

_____

_____

_____

☐ MOTOR TIMING BELT ☐ AIR CONDITIONING ☐ LIGHTING _____

DATE _____ MILES OR KILOMETERS _____

☐ REPAIR

SERVICE REPORT

☐ INSPECTION

☐ MAINTENANCE

☐ SERVICE   ☐ BIG   ☐ SMALL   ☐ ENTER EXTRA WORK ABOVE

☐ ENGINE OIL CHANGE/BRAND/VISCOSITY _____

☐ OIL FILTER CHANGE/BRAND _____

☐ ENGINE OIL CONTROL   ☐ OKAY   ☐ REFILLED _____

☐ TRANSMISSION ÖL CONTROL   ☐ OKAY   ☐ EXCHANGED _____

☐ SPARK PLUGS   ☐ CONTROL OKAY   ☐ EXCHANGED _____

☐ GLOW PLUGS   ☐ CONTROL OKAY   ☐ EXCHANGED _____

☐ BRAKES   ☐ CONTROL OKAY   ☐ REPAIRED   ☐ EXCHANGED _____

☐ BRAKE FLUID   ☐ CONTROL OKAY   ☐ EXCHANGED _____

☐ COOLANT   ☐ CONTROL OKAY   ☐ EXCHANGED _____

☐ MORE WORK _____

DATE OF NEXT SERVICE _____
OR MILES/KILOMETERS _____

SIGNATURE _____

STAMP

EXTRA WORK _____ **AIR PRESSURE**

_____

_____

_____

☐ **PARKING CONTROL**   ☐ **UPDATE NAVIGATION**   ☐ **MEASURE AXES**   ☐ **INTERIOR CLEANING**

AUTO BODY WORK   ☐ **NEW PARTS**   ☐ **REPAIRED**

_____

_____

_____

_____

_____

_____

☐ **MOTOR TIMING BELT**   ☐ **AIR CONDITIONING**   ☐ **LIGHTING** _____

DATE _____ MILES OR KILOMETERS _____

☐ REPAIR
☐ INSPECTION
☐ MAINTENANCE

SERVICE REPORT

☐ SERVICE ☐ BIG ☐ SMALL ☐ ENTER EXTRA WORK ABOVE

☐ ENGINE OIL CHANGE/BRAND/VISCOSITY _____

☐ OIL FILTER CHANGE/BRAND _____

☐ ENGINE OIL CONTROL ☐ OKAY ☐ REFILLED _____

☐ TRANSMISSION ÖL CONTROL ☐ OKAY ☐ EXCHANGED

☐ SPARK PLUGS ☐ CONTROL OKAY ☐ EXCHANGED _____

☐ GLOW PLUGS ☐ CONTROL OKAY ☐ EXCHANGED _____

☐ BRAKES ☐ CONTROL OKAY ☐ REPAIRED ☐ EXCHANGED _____

☐ BRAKE FLUID ☐ CONTROL OKAY ☐ EXCHANGED _____

☐ COOLANT ☐ CONTROL OKAY ☐ EXCHANGED _____

☐ MORE WORK _____

DATE OF NEXT SERVICE _____
OR MILES/KILOMETERS _____

STAMP

SIGNATURE _____

EXTRA WORK _____ **AIR PRESSURE**

_____

_____

☐ **PARKING CONTROL**   ☐ **UPDATE NAVIGATION**   ☐ **MEASURE AXES**   ☐ **INTERIOR CLEANING**

AUTO BODY WORK   ☐ **NEW PARTS**   ☐ **REPAIRED**

_____

_____

_____

_____

_____

☐ **MOTOR TIMING BELT**   ☐ **AIR CONDITIONING**   ☐ **LIGHTING** _____

DATE _____   MILES OR KILOMETERS _____   ☐ REPAIR

SERVICE REPORT

☐ INSPECTION

☐ MAINTENANCE

☐ SERVICE   ☐ BIG   ☐ SMALL   ☐ ENTER EXTRA WORK ABOVE

☐ ENGINE OIL CHANGE/BRAND/VISCOSITY _____

☐ OIL FILTER CHANGE/BRAND _____

☐ ENGINE OIL CONTROL   ☐ OKAY   ☐ REFILLED   _____

☐ TRANSMISSION ÖL CONTROL   ☐ OKAY   ☐ EXCHANGED   _____

☐ SPARK PLUGS   ☐ CONTROL OKAY   ☐ EXCHANGED   _____

☐ GLOW PLUGS   ☐ CONTROL OKAY   ☐ EXCHANGED _____

☐ BRAKES   ☐ CONTROL OKAY   ☐ REPAIRED   ☐ EXCHANGED _____

☐ BRAKE FLUID   ☐ CONTROL OKAY   ☐ EXCHANGED _____

☐ COOLANT   ☐ CONTROL OKAY   ☐ EXCHANGED _____

☐ MORE WORK _____

DATE OF NEXT SERVICE ————————————
OR MILES/KILOMETERS ————————————

SIGNATURE _____

STAMP

EXTRA WORK _____ AIR PRESSURE

_____

_____

☐ PARKING CONTROL   ☐ UPDATE NAVIGATION   ☐ MEASURE AXES   ☐ INTERIOR CLEANING

AUTO BODY WORK   ☐ NEW PARTS   ☐ REPAIRED

_____

_____

_____

_____

_____

_____

☐ MOTOR TIMING BELT   ☐ AIR CONDITIONING   ☐ LIGHTING _____

DATE _____

MILES OR
KILOMETERS _____

☐ REPAIR

☐ INSPECTION

SERVICE REPORT

☐ MAINTENANCE

☐ SERVICE   ☐ BIG   ☐ SMALL   ☐ ENTER EXTRA
                                              WORK ABOVE

☐ ENGINE OIL CHANGE/BRAND/VISCOSITY _____

☐ OIL FILTER CHANGE/BRAND _____

☐ ENGINE OIL CONTROL   ☐ OKAY   ☐ REFILLED   _____

☐ TRANSMISSION ÖL   ☐ OKAY   ☐ EXCHANGED   _____
   CONTROL

☐ SPARK PLUGS   ☐ CONTROL OKAY ☐ EXCHANGED _____

☐ GLOW PLUGS   ☐ CONTROL OKAY ☐ EXCHANGED _____

☐ BRAKES   ☐ CONTROL OKAY ☐ REPAIRED   ☐ EXCHANGED _____

☐ BRAKE FLUID   ☐ CONTROL OKAY   ☐ EXCHANGED _____

☐ COOLANT   ☐ CONTROL OKAY   ☐ EXCHANGED _____

☐ MORE WORK _____

DATE OF NEXT SERVICE _____
OR MILES/KILOMETERS _____

STAMP

SIGNATURE _____

EXTRA WORK _____ **AIR PRESSURE**

_____

_____

_____

☐ **PARKING CONTROL**   ☐ **UPDATE NAVIGATION**   ☐ **MEASURE AXES**   ☐ **INTERIOR CLEANING**

AUTO BODY WORK   ☐ **NEW PARTS**   ☐ **REPAIRED**

_____

_____

_____

_____

_____

☐ **MOTOR TIMING BELT**   ☐ **AIR CONDITIONING**   ☐ **LIGHTING** _____

DATE _____ MILES OR KILOMETERS _____

☐ REPAIR

SERVICE REPORT

☐ INSPECTION

☐ MAINTENANCE

☐ SERVICE   ☐ BIG   ☐ SMALL   ☐ ENTER EXTRA WORK ABOVE

☐ ENGINE OIL CHANGE/BRAND/VISCOSITY _____

☐ OIL FILTER CHANGE/BRAND _____

☐ ENGINE OIL CONTROL   ☐ OKAY   ☐ REFILLED   _____

☐ TRANSMISSION ÖL CONTROL   ☐ OKAY   ☐ EXCHANGED   _____

☐ SPARK PLUGS   ☐ CONTROL OKAY   ☐ EXCHANGED   _____

☐ GLOW PLUGS   ☐ CONTROL OKAY   ☐ EXCHANGED   _____

☐ BRAKES   ☐ CONTROL OKAY   ☐ REPAIRED   ☐ EXCHANGED _____

☐ BRAKE FLUID   ☐ CONTROL OKAY   ☐ EXCHANGED   _____

☐ COOLANT   ☐ CONTROL OKAY   ☐ EXCHANGED   _____

☐ MORE WORK _____

DATE OF NEXT SERVICE _____
OR MILES/KILOMETERS _____

SIGNATURE _____

┌─────────────────────────┐
│ STAMP   │
│   │
│   │
│   │
│   │
└─────────────────────────┘

EXTRA WORK _____ **AIR PRESSURE**

_____

_____

_____

☐ **PARKING CONTROL**   ☐ **UPDATE NAVIGATION**   ☐ **MEASURE AXES**   ☐ **INTERIOR CLEANING**

AUTO BODY WORK   ☐ **NEW PARTS**   ☐ **REPAIRED**

_____

_____

_____

_____

_____

_____

☐ **MOTOR TIMING BELT**   ☐ **AIR CONDITIONING**   ☐ **LIGHTING** _____

DATE _____   MILES OR KILOMETERS _____   ☐ REPAIR

SERVICE REPORT

☐ INSPECTION

☐ MAINTENANCE

☐ SERVICE   ☐ BIG   ☐ SMALL   ☐ ENTER EXTRA WORK ABOVE

☐ ENGINE OIL CHANGE/BRAND/VISCOSITY _____

☐ OIL FILTER CHANGE/BRAND _____

☐ ENGINE OIL CONTROL   ☐ OKAY   ☐ REFILLED _____

☐ TRANSMISSION ÖL CONTROL   ☐ OKAY   ☐ EXCHANGED _____

☐ SPARK PLUGS   ☐ CONTROL OKAY   ☐ EXCHANGED _____

☐ GLOW PLUGS   ☐ CONTROL OKAY   ☐ EXCHANGED _____

☐ BRAKES   ☐ CONTROL OKAY   ☐ REPAIRED   ☐ EXCHANGED _____

☐ BRAKE FLUID   ☐ CONTROL OKAY   ☐ EXCHANGED _____

☐ COOLANT   ☐ CONTROL OKAY   ☐ EXCHANGED _____

☐ MORE WORK _____

DATE OF NEXT SERVICE _____
OR MILES/KILOMETERS _____

STAMP

SIGNATURE _____

EXTRA WORK _____ AIR PRESSURE

_____

_____

_____

_____

☐ PARKING CONTROL   ☐ UPDATE NAVIGATION   ☐ MEASURE AXES   ☐ INTERIOR CLEANING

AUTO BODY WORK   ☐ NEW PARTS   ☐ REPAIRED

_____

_____

_____

_____

_____

_____

☐ MOTOR TIMING BELT   ☐ AIR CONDITIONING   ☐ LIGHTING _____

DATE _____   MILES OR KILOMETERS _____   ☐ REPAIR

SERVICE REPORT

☐ INSPECTION

☐ MAINTENANCE

☐ SERVICE   ☐ BIG   ☐ SMALL   ☐ ENTER EXTRA WORK ABOVE

☐ ENGINE OIL CHANGE/BRAND/VISCOSITY _____

☐ OIL FILTER CHANGE/BRAND _____

☐ ENGINE OIL CONTROL   ☐ OKAY   ☐ REFILLED _____

☐ TRANSMISSION ÖL CONTROL   ☐ OKAY   ☐ EXCHANGED _____

☐ SPARK PLUGS   ☐ CONTROL OKAY   ☐ EXCHANGED _____

☐ GLOW PLUGS   ☐ CONTROL OKAY   ☐ EXCHANGED _____

☐ BRAKES   ☐ CONTROL OKAY   ☐ REPAIRED   ☐ EXCHANGED _____

☐ BRAKE FLUID   ☐ CONTROL OKAY   ☐ EXCHANGED _____

☐ COOLANT   ☐ CONTROL OKAY   ☐ EXCHANGED _____

☐ MORE WORK _____

DATE OF NEXT SERVICE OR MILES/KILOMETERS _____

STAMP

SIGNATURE _____

EXTRA WORK _____ **AIR PRESSURE**

_____

_____

_____

☐ **PARKING CONTROL** ☐ **UPDATE NAVIGATION** ☐ **MEASURE AXES** ☐ **INTERIOR CLEANING**

AUTO BODY WORK ☐ **NEW PARTS** ☐ **REPAIRED**

_____

_____

_____

_____

_____

_____

☐ **MOTOR TIMING BELT** ☐ **AIR CONDITIONING** ☐ **LIGHTING** _____

DATE _____

MILES OR
KILOMETERS _____

SERVICE REPORT

☐ REPAIR

☐ INSPECTION

☐ MAINTENANCE

☐ SERVICE ☐ BIG ☐ SMALL ☐ ENTER EXTRA WORK ABOVE

☐ ENGINE OIL CHANGE/BRAND/VISCOSITY _____

☐ OIL FILTER CHANGE/BRAND _____

☐ ENGINE OIL CONTROL ☐ OKAY ☐ REFILLED _____

☐ TRANSMISSION ÖL CONTROL ☐ OKAY ☐ EXCHANGED _____

☐ SPARK PLUGS ☐ CONTROL OKAY ☐ EXCHANGED _____

☐ GLOW PLUGS ☐ CONTROL OKAY ☐ EXCHANGED _____

☐ BRAKES ☐ CONTROL OKAY ☐ REPAIRED ☐ EXCHANGED _____

☐ BRAKE FLUID ☐ CONTROL OKAY ☐ EXCHANGED _____

☐ COOLANT ☐ CONTROL OKAY ☐ EXCHANGED _____

☐ MORE WORK

DATE OF NEXT SERVICE
OR MILES/KILOMETERS _____

SIGNATURE _____

STAMP

EXTRA WORK _____ **AIR PRESSURE**

_____

_____

_____

☐ **PARKING CONTROL** ☐ **UPDATE NAVIGATION** ☐ **MEASURE AXES** ☐ **INTERIOR CLEANING**

AUTO BODY WORK ☐ **NEW PARTS** ☐ **REPAIRED**

_____

_____

_____

_____

_____

_____

☐ **MOTOR TIMING BELT** ☐ **AIR CONDITIONING** ☐ **LIGHTING** _____

DATE _____ MILES OR
KILOMETERS _____

SERVICE REPORT

☐ REPAIR

☐ INSPECTION

☐ MAINTENANCE

☐ SERVICE   ☐ BIG   ☐ SMALL   ☐ ENTER EXTRA WORK ABOVE

☐ ENGINE OIL CHANGE/BRAND/VISCOSITY _____

☐ OIL FILTER CHANGE/BRAND _____

☐ ENGINE OIL CONTROL   ☐ OKAY   ☐ REFILLED   _____

☐ TRANSMISSION ÖL CONTROL   ☐ OKAY   ☐ EXCHANGED   _____

☐ SPARK PLUGS   ☐ CONTROL OKAY   ☐ EXCHANGED   _____

☐ GLOW PLUGS   ☐ CONTROL OKAY   ☐ EXCHANGED   _____

☐ BRAKES   ☐ CONTROL OKAY   ☐ REPAIRED   ☐ EXCHANGED   _____

☐ BRAKE FLUID   ☐ CONTROL OKAY   ☐ EXCHANGED   _____

☐ COOLANT   ☐ CONTROL OKAY   ☐ EXCHANGED   _____

☐ MORE WORK _____

DATE OF NEXT SERVICE _____
OR MILES/KILOMETERS _____

SIGNATURE _____

STAMP

EXTRA WORK _____ AIR PRESSURE

_____

_____

_____

☐ **PARKING CONTROL**   ☐ **UPDATE NAVIGATION**   ☐ **MEASURE AXES**   ☐ **INTERIOR CLEANING**

AUTO BODY WORK   ☐ **NEW PARTS**   ☐ **REPAIRED**

_____

_____

_____

_____

_____

_____

☐ **MOTOR TIMING BELT**   ☐ **AIR CONDITIONING**   ☐ **LIGHTING** _____

DATE _____ MILES OR
KILOMETERS _____

☐ REPAIR

SERVICE REPORT

☐ INSPECTION

☐ MAINTENANCE

☐ SERVICE   ☐ BIG   ☐ SMALL   ☐ ENTER EXTRA
                                          WORK ABOVE

☐ ENGINE OIL CHANGE/BRAND/VISCOSITY _____

☐ OIL FILTER CHANGE/BRAND _____

☐ ENGINE OIL CONTROL   ☐ OKAY   ☐ REFILLED _____

☐ TRANSMISSION ÖL CONTROL   ☐ OKAY   ☐ EXCHANGED _____

☐ SPARK PLUGS   ☐ CONTROL OKAY   ☐ EXCHANGED _____

☐ GLOW PLUGS   ☐ CONTROL OKAY   ☐ EXCHANGED _____

☐ BRAKES   ☐ CONTROL OKAY   ☐ REPAIRED   ☐ EXCHANGED _____

☐ BRAKE FLUID   ☐ CONTROL OKAY   ☐ EXCHANGED _____

☐ COOLANT   ☐ CONTROL OKAY   ☐ EXCHANGED _____

☐ MORE WORK _____

DATE OF NEXT SERVICE _____
OR MILES/KILOMETERS _____

STAMP

SIGNATURE _____

EXTRA WORK _____ AIR PRESSURE

_____

_____

_____

☐ PARKING CONTROL ☐ UPDATE NAVIGATION ☐ MEASURE AXES ☐ INTERIOR CLEANING

AUTO BODY WORK ☐ NEW PARTS ☐ REPAIRED

_____

_____

_____

_____

_____

_____

☐ MOTOR TIMING BELT ☐ AIR CONDITIONING ☐ LIGHTING _____

DATE _____   MILES OR KILOMETERS _____   ☐ REPAIR

SERVICE REPORT
☐ INSPECTION

☐ MAINTENANCE

☐ SERVICE   ☐ BIG   ☐ SMALL   ☐ **ENTER EXTRA WORK ABOVE**

☐ ENGINE OIL CHANGE/BRAND/VISCOSITY _____

☐ OIL FILTER CHANGE/BRAND _____

☐ ENGINE OIL CONTROL   ☐ OKAY   ☐ REFILLED _____

☐ TRANSMISSION ÖL CONTROL   ☐ OKAY   ☐ EXCHANGED _____

☐ SPARK PLUGS   ☐ CONTROL OKAY   ☐ EXCHANGED _____

☐ GLOW PLUGS   ☐ CONTROL OKAY   ☐ EXCHANGED _____

☐ BRAKES   ☐ CONTROL OKAY   ☐ REPAIRED   ☐ EXCHANGED _____

☐ BRAKE FLUID   ☐ CONTROL OKAY   ☐ EXCHANGED _____

☐ COOLANT   ☐ CONTROL OKAY   ☐ EXCHANGED _____

☐ MORE WORK _____

DATE OF NEXT SERVICE _____
OR MILES/KILOMETERS _____

SIGNATURE _____

STAMP

EXTRA WORK _____ AIR PRESSURE

_____ ____ ____

_____ ____ ____

_____

☐ PARKING CONTROL ☐ UPDATE NAVIGATION ☐ MEASURE AXES ☐ INTERIOR CLEANING

AUTO BODY WORK ☐ NEW PARTS ☐ REPAIRED

_____

_____

_____

_____

_____

_____

☐ MOTOR TIMING BELT ☐ AIR CONDITIONING ☐ LIGHTING _____

DATE _____ 　MILES OR
KILOMETERS _____

☐ REPAIR

☐ INSPECTION

SERVICE REPORT

☐ MAINTENANCE

☐ SERVICE　　☐ BIG　　☐ SMALL　☐ ENTER EXTRA
　　　　　　　　　　　　　　　　　　　WORK ABOVE

☐ ENGINE OIL CHANGE/BRAND/VISCOSITY _____

☐ OIL FILTER CHANGE/BRAND _____

☐ ENGINE OIL CONTROL　☐ OKAY　☐ REFILLED _____

☐ TRANSMISSION ÖL
　　CONTROL　☐ OKAY　☐ EXCHANGED _____

☐ SPARK PLUGS　☐ CONTROL OKAY　☐ EXCHANGED _____

☐ GLOW PLUGS　☐ CONTROL OKAY　☐ EXCHANGED _____

☐ BRAKES　☐ CONTROL OKAY　☐ REPAIRED　☐ EXCHANGED _____

☐ BRAKE FLUID　☐ CONTROL OKAY　☐ EXCHANGED _____

☐ COOLANT　☐ CONTROL OKAY　☐ EXCHANGED _____

☐ MORE WORK _____

DATE OF NEXT SERVICE _____
OR MILES/KILOMETERS _____

STAMP

SIGNATURE _____

EXTRA WORK _____ AIR PRESSURE

_____

_____

_____

☐ PARKING CONTROL   ☐ UPDATE NAVIGATION   ☐ MEASURE AXES   ☐ INTERIOR CLEANING

AUTO BODY WORK   ☐ NEW PARTS   ☐ REPAIRED

_____

_____

_____

_____

_____

_____

☐ MOTOR TIMING BELT   ☐ AIR CONDITIONING   ☐ LIGHTING _____

DATE _____

MILES OR
KILOMETERS _____

☐ REPAIR

☐ INSPECTION

SERVICE REPORT

☐ MAINTENANCE

☐ SERVICE   ☐ BIG   ☐ SMALL   ☐ ENTER EXTRA
WORK ABOVE

☐ ENGINE OIL CHANGE/BRAND/VISCOSITY _____

☐ OIL FILTER CHANGE/BRAND _____

☐ ENGINE OIL CONTROL   ☐ OKAY   ☐ REFILLED _____

☐ TRANSMISSION ÖL CONTROL   ☐ OKAY   ☐ EXCHANGED _____

☐ SPARK PLUGS   ☐ CONTROL OKAY   ☐ EXCHANGED _____

☐ GLOW PLUGS   ☐ CONTROL OKAY   ☐ EXCHANGED _____

☐ BRAKES   ☐ CONTROL OKAY   ☐ REPAIRED   ☐ EXCHANGED _____

☐ BRAKE FLUID   ☐ CONTROL OKAY   ☐ EXCHANGED _____

☐ COOLANT   ☐ CONTROL OKAY   ☐ EXCHANGED _____

☐ MORE WORK _____

DATE OF NEXT SERVICE _____
OR MILES/KILOMETERS _____

SIGNATURE _____

STAMP

EXTRA WORK _____ AIR PRESSURE

_____

_____

_____

☐ PARKING CONTROL ☐ UPDATE NAVIGATION ☐ MEASURE AXES ☐ INTERIOR CLEANING

AUTO BODY WORK ☐ NEW PARTS ☐ REPAIRED

_____

_____

_____

_____

_____

_____

☐ MOTOR TIMING BELT ☐ AIR CONDITIONING ☐ LIGHTING _____

DATE _____ MILES OR KILOMETERS _____

☐ REPAIR

☐ INSPECTION

SERVICE REPORT

☐ MAINTENANCE

☐ SERVICE ☐ BIG ☐ SMALL ☐ ENTER EXTRA WORK ABOVE

☐ ENGINE OIL CHANGE/BRAND/VISCOSITY _____

☐ OIL FILTER CHANGE/BRAND _____

☐ ENGINE OIL CONTROL ☐ OKAY ☐ REFILLED _____

☐ TRANSMISSION ÖL CONTROL ☐ OKAY ☐ EXCHANGED _____

☐ SPARK PLUGS ☐ CONTROL OKAY ☐ EXCHANGED _____

☐ GLOW PLUGS ☐ CONTROL OKAY ☐ EXCHANGED _____

☐ BRAKES ☐ CONTROL OKAY ☐ REPAIRED ☐ EXCHANGED _____

☐ BRAKE FLUID ☐ CONTROL OKAY ☐ EXCHANGED _____

☐ COOLANT ☐ CONTROL OKAY ☐ EXCHANGED _____

☐ MORE WORK _____

DATE OF NEXT SERVICE _____
OR MILES/KILOMETERS _____

STAMP

SIGNATURE _____

EXTRA WORK _____ AIR PRESSURE

_____

_____

_____

☐ PARKING CONTROL ☐ UPDATE NAVIGATION ☐ MEASURE AXES ☐ INTERIOR CLEANING

AUTO BODY WORK ☐ NEW PARTS ☐ REPAIRED

_____

_____

_____

_____

_____

_____

☐ MOTOR TIMING BELT ☐ AIR CONDITIONING ☐ LIGHTING _____

DATE _____
MILES OR
KILOMETERS _____

☐ REPAIR

SERVICE REPORT

☐ INSPECTION

☐ MAINTENANCE

☐ SERVICE   ☐ BIG   ☐ SMALL   ☐ ENTER EXTRA WORK ABOVE

☐ ENGINE OIL CHANGE/BRAND/VISCOSITY _____

☐ OIL FILTER CHANGE/BRAND _____

☐ ENGINE OIL CONTROL   ☐ OKAY   ☐ REFILLED _____

☐ TRANSMISSION ÖL CONTROL   ☐ OKAY   ☐ EXCHANGED _____

☐ SPARK PLUGS   ☐ CONTROL OKAY   ☐ EXCHANGED _____

☐ GLOW PLUGS   ☐ CONTROL OKAY   ☐ EXCHANGED _____

☐ BRAKES   ☐ CONTROL OKAY   ☐ REPAIRED   ☐ EXCHANGED _____

☐ BRAKE FLUID   ☐ CONTROL OKAY   ☐ EXCHANGED _____

☐ COOLANT   ☐ CONTROL OKAY   ☐ EXCHANGED _____

☐ MORE WORK

DATE OF NEXT SERVICE _____
OR MILES/KILOMETERS _____

STAMP

SIGNATURE _____

EXTRA WORK _____ **AIR PRESSURE**

_____

_____

_____

☐ **PARKING CONTROL** ☐ **UPDATE NAVIGATION** ☐ **MEASURE AXES** ☐ **INTERIOR CLEANING**

AUTO BODY WORK ☐ **NEW PARTS** ☐ **REPAIRED**

_____

_____

_____

_____

_____

_____

☐ **MOTOR TIMING BELT** ☐ **AIR CONDITIONING** ☐ **LIGHTING** _____

DATE _____ MILES OR KILOMETERS _____ ☐ REPAIR

SERVICE REPORT
☐ INSPECTION
☐ MAINTENANCE

☐ SERVICE   ☐ BIG   ☐ SMALL ☐ ENTER EXTRA WORK ABOVE

☐ ENGINE OIL CHANGE/BRAND/VISCOSITY _____

☐ OIL FILTER CHANGE/BRAND _____

☐ ENGINE OIL CONTROL ☐ OKAY ☐ REFILLED _____

☐ TRANSMISSION ÖL CONTROL ☐ OKAY ☐ EXCHANGED _____

☐ SPARK PLUGS ☐ CONTROL OKAY ☐ EXCHANGED _____

☐ GLOW PLUGS ☐ CONTROL OKAY ☐ EXCHANGED _____

☐ BRAKES ☐ CONTROL OKAY ☐ REPAIRED ☐ EXCHANGED _____

☐ BRAKE FLUID ☐ CONTROL OKAY ☐ EXCHANGED _____

☐ COOLANT ☐ CONTROL OKAY ☐ EXCHANGED _____

☐ MORE WORK

DATE OF NEXT SERVICE _____
OR MILES/KILOMETERS _____

STAMP

SIGNATURE _____

EXTRA WORK _____ AIR PRESSURE

_____

_____

_____

☐ PARKING CONTROL   ☐ UPDATE NAVIGATION   ☐ MEASURE AXES   ☐ INTERIOR CLEANING

AUTO BODY WORK   ☐ NEW PARTS   ☐ REPAIRED

_____

_____

_____

_____

_____

_____

☐ MOTOR TIMING BELT   ☐ AIR CONDITIONING   ☐ LIGHTING _____

DATE _____ MILES OR
KILOMETERS _____ ☐ REPAIR

SERVICE REPORT
☐ INSPECTION

☐ MAINTENANCE

☐ SERVICE   ☐ BIG   ☐ SMALL   ☐ ENTER EXTRA
                                     WORK ABOVE

☐ ENGINE OIL CHANGE/BRAND/VISCOSITY _____

☐ OIL FILTER CHANGE/BRAND _____

☐ ENGINE OIL CONTROL   ☐ OKAY   ☐ REFILLED _____

☐ TRANSMISSION ÖL
   CONTROL   ☐ OKAY   ☐ EXCHANGED _____

☐ SPARK PLUGS   ☐ CONTROL OKAY   ☐ EXCHANGED _____

☐ GLOW PLUGS   ☐ CONTROL OKAY   ☐ EXCHANGED _____

☐ BRAKES   ☐ CONTROL OKAY   ☐ REPAIRED   ☐ EXCHANGED _____

☐ BRAKE FLUID   ☐ CONTROL OKAY   ☐ EXCHANGED _____

☐ COOLANT   ☐ CONTROL OKAY   ☐ EXCHANGED _____

☐ MORE WORK _____

DATE OF NEXT SERVICE _____
OR MILES/KILOMETERS _____

STAMP

SIGNATURE _____

GAS STATION

GASOLINE BOOKLET

NOTES FOR DATE, MILES, GALLONS, PRICE PER GALLON, GAS TYPE AND AIR PRESSURE

Snelltz Books
INTERNATIONAL